How Does My Home Work?
Electricity

Chris Oxlade

Heinemann
LIBRARY
Chicago, Illinois

www.capstonepub.com
Visit our website to find out more information about Heinemann-Raintree books.

To order:

☎ Phone 800-747-4992

💻 Visit www.capstonepub.com to browse our catalog and order online.

Edited by Daniel Nunn, Rebecca Rissman, and Catherine Veitch
Designed by Joanna Hinton-Malivoire
Picture research by Elizabeth Alexander
Production by Alison Parsons
Originated by Capstone Global Library Ltd
Printed and bound in China by Leo Paper Products

16 15 14 13 12
10 9 8 7 6 5 4 3 2 1

Library of Congress Cataloging-in-Publication Data
Oxlade, Chris.
  Electricity / Chris Oxlade.
      p. cm.—(How does my home work?)
  Includes bibliographical references and index.
  ISBN 978-1-4329-6565-5 (hb)—ISBN 978-1-4329-6570-9 (pb)
1. Electricity—Juvenile literature. I. Title.
  QC527.2.O947 2013
  621.319'24—dc23   2011038248

Acknowledgments
We would like to thank the following for permission to reproduce photographs: Alamy pp. 8 (© Harry Sheridan), 9 (Ted Foxx), 16 (© Matthew Kirwan); Corbis p. 20 (© Ocean); iStockphoto pp. 15 (© Matthew Brown) 23 (© Matthew Brown); Shutterstock pp. 4 (© Harry Hu), 5 (© Jozef Sedmak), 6 (© yampi), 7 (© Monkey Business Images), 10 (© Mark William Richardson), 11 (© Yegor Korzh), 12 (© Zeljko Radojko), 13 (© Tungphoto), 14 (© Yellowj), 17 (© Mark Herreid), 18 (© Nick Hawkes), 19 (© anyaivanova), 21 (© Monika Wisniewska), 23 (© Yellowj, © THP | Tim Hester Photography, © Harry Hu, © Monkey Business Images, © Nick Hawkes, © Tungphoto).

Cover photograph of an energy-efficient lightbulb reproduced with permission of Shutterstock (© Sideways Design). Background photograph of vector lights reproduced with permission of Shutterstock (© Kundra).

Back cover photographs of (left) a power station reproduced with permission of Shutterstock (© Mark William Richardson), and (right) a lightbulb reproduced with permission of Shutterstock (© Mark Herreid).

Every effort has been made to contact copyright holders of material reproduced in this book. Any omissions will be rectified in subsequent printings if notice is given to the publisher.

We would like to thank Terence Alexander for his invaluable help in the preparation of this book.

Disclaimer
All the Internet addresses (URLs) given in this book were valid at the time of going to press. However, due to the dynamic nature of the Internet, some addresses may have changed, or sites may have changed or ceased to exist since publication. While the author and Publishers regret any inconvenience this may cause readers, no responsibility for any such changes can be accepted by either the author or the Publishers.

Contents

Some words are shown in bold, **like this**. You can
find them in the glossary on page 23.

What Is Electricity?

Electricity makes lights and other things in our homes work.

Electricity is a kind of **energy**.

Most homes have electricity.

We can use electricity to make light, heat, and sound.

Where Do We Use Electricity at Home?

Electricity powers all sorts of machines in your home.

Can you name some of the machines electricity powers in this kitchen?

Electricity also powers many **gadgets** we use at home.

Electricity powers the control for this boy's game console.

Is Electricity Dangerous?

safety cover

Household electricity can injure or even kill a person.

Never play with electric plugs or **outlets**.

This is a special safety plug.

If anything goes wrong, the plug switches the electricity off.

Where Is Electricity Made?

Some electricity is made at power stations like this one.

Power stations burn coal, oil, or gas to make electricity.

wind turbine

These machines are called wind turbines.

Wind turbines turn the **energy** from wind into electricity.

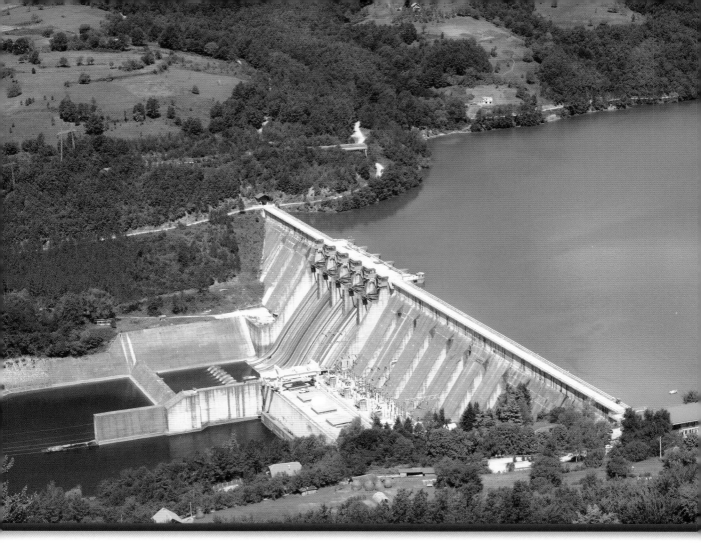

This is a hydroelectric power station.

The **energy** from water rushing downhill is turned into electricity.

power line

Electricity travels along **power lines** to towns and cities.

Cables under the street or on tall poles take the electricity to your home.

How Does Electricity Get Around My Home?

Electricity travels around your home along wires and **cables**.

The wires and cables are buried in the walls and under the floors.

outlet

plug

The cables carry electricity to **outlets** in the walls.

To make a machine work you put its plug into an outlet.

How Do Electric Lights Work?

Cables carry electricity to the lights in your home.

Light switches turn the electricity to the lights on and off.

lightbulb

A lightbulb turns electricity into light.

When electricity flows into the bulb, the bulb glows brightly.

Does Electricity Harm Our Planet?

pollution

Burning materials such as coal, oil, and gas makes **pollution** in the air.

This causes a problem with our weather called **climate change**.

This power station makes electricity from sunshine instead.

This means we do not have to burn so much coal, oil, or gas.

How Can We Use Less Electricity?

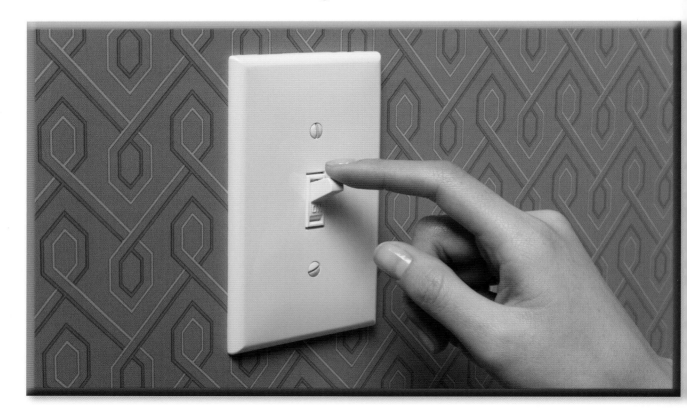

We can help our planet by using less electricity.

For example, you can switch off lights when you do not need them.

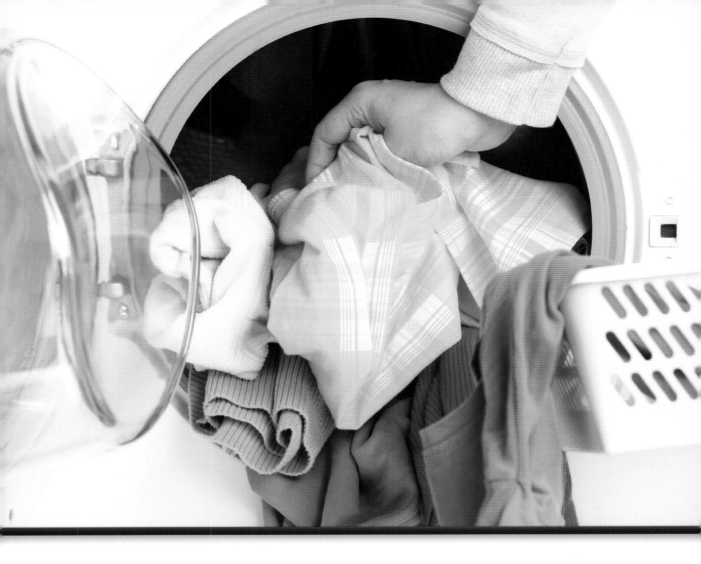

Make sure your washing machine is full each time you use it.

Also, wash clothes at a lower heat to save electricity.

Saving Electricity Poster

Is your family good at saving electricity?

Make a poster to stick on your refrigerator, like this one, to remind people what to do.

How To Save Electricity

- Switch off the lights when you leave a room.
- Turn off the television when you are not watching it.
- Shut down the computer when you are not using it.
- Turn down the heat. Wear a sweater!
- Fill the washing machine up before you turn it on.
- Only boil as much water as you need.

Glossary

 **cable** tube with wires inside that carry electricity

 **climate change** changes to the weather that happen in different parts of the world

 **energy** power that is needed to make things move, change, or grow

 **gadget** small machine

 **outlet** special holes in the wall where you can plug in an electric machine

 **pollution** harmful things in the air, water, or soil. It is caused by humans.

 **power line** thick cable that carries electricity from a power station to homes

Find Out More

Books

Alpert, Barbara. *Electricity All Around.* Mankato, MN: Capstone Publishers, 2012.

Oxlade, Chris. *Investigate: Electricity.* Chicago: Heinemann Library, 2009.

Website

www.energystar.gov/index.cfm?c=kids.kids_index
Play games and learn more about energy at this website.

Index